GERMANY
WITHIN THE BOUNDARIES OF 1937

The places marked by a full dot
on the map are represented by
illustrations in the book.

OSTSEE

KÖNIGSBERG

Memel

Trakehnen

under Russian

under Polish administration

Rominten Heath

DANTZIG

Elbing

Marienburg

Stolp

Stolpe

Persante

Rega

Weichsel

STETTIN

under Polish administration

Chorin

Oder

Netze

Warthe

BERLIN

Spree

Potsdam

Spreewald

Frankfort

Oder

Grünberg

Bober

Bartsch

Militsch

Gr.
Wartenberg

Leubus

Oder

BRESLAU

Stober

Kreuzburg

Liegnitz

Bunzlau

under Polish administration

Malapane

Görlitz

Neisse

Meissen

DRESDEN

Hirschberg

Waldenburg

Schweidnitz

Oppeln

Oder

Beuthen

Freiberg

Gebirge

Sudeten

Neisse

Neisse

Gleiwitz

Glatz

Ratibor

EAST PRUSSIA

POMERANIA

MECKLENBURG

BRANDENBURG

BERLIN

SILESIA

SAXONY

THURINGIA

Bavarian Forest

Danube

Ilz

Passau

Inn

Berchtesgaden

Königssee

GERMANY

Countryside, Cities, Villages and People

16 COLOUR PLATES, 228 FULL-PAGE PHOTOGRAPHS
BY GERMANY'S LEADING PHOTOGRAPHERS

UMSCHAU VERLAG · FRANKFURT AM MAIN

INTRODUCTION BY RUDOLF HAGELSTANGE

PICTURE CAPTIONS BY HARALD BUSCH

15TH EDITION

© 1956 BY UMSCHAU VERLAG, FRANKFURT AM MAIN · PRINTED IN GERMANY

EDITORS: DR. HARALD BUSCH AND DR. H. BREIDENSTEIN, FRANKFURT AM MAIN

JACKET DESIGN BY HANS BREIDENSTEIN, FRANKFURT AM MAIN

PRINTED AND BOUND BY BRÖNNERS DRUCKEREI (BREIDENSTEIN), FRANKFURT AM MAIN

LIST OF ILLUSTRATIONS

in Alphabetical Order

There are many countries in the world and it is only natural for each of us to rate his native land above all others. The Germans, too, like to praise their beautiful homeland. Many visitors from other lands will understand and share these feelings. Germany has always attracted visitors by reason of the diversity of the countryside and by the sympathy, friendliness and hospitality of her people. Enjoying a central position and open to influences from east, west, north and south, the German towns, especially Berlin, offered a second home to many people of other nations. It was and is even today an essential feature of the German character to be open to others.

This is, of course, hardly surprising. Germany grew up into a nation rather late in the day, in face of strong opposition from the separate states, jealously guarding their own individuality. Denmark is nearer to a Schleswiger than Bavaria. A Düsseldorfer finds it more charming to go to Paris over the weekend than to Berlin. And between a vintner of the Moselle and a peasant of the Erzgebirge, the difference of character might easily justify the setting up of a frontier. This very variety, however, which makes it so difficult for Germany to achieve political unity is a source of richness.

Before the outcome of the second World War was so disastrous for Germany, this variety was to be found within a large frame. Today this frame has been hacked to pieces. The terms Silesia and East Prussia are still used, but are they still living conceptions? It is always the East Prussia or the Silesia of the past that is meant. Germany has been torn asunder by the fortunes of war, but surely Germany does not end behind the iron curtain. Surely every German has the right to expect that the two halves will soon be welded together again and that the peoples, different as they are in character, will soon be able to live together in freedom and harmony.

The traveller standing on a peak of the Alps must imagine Germany to be a long staircase gently sloping down to the sea, washing her northern shores. From the Rhine bend near Basle down to the Königssee near Berchtesgaden stretches the mountain barrier between north and south. In the valleys nestle the most charming little towns in S. Germany; the waters of the Bavarian lakes and of Lake Constance wash the foothills of the Alps. This soil nurtures very headstrong people, opposed to all conformity. Their national costumes are not decorative pieces meant to be admired in the wardrobe; they are intended for daily wear. The Sunday morning procession of church-goers in the Black Forest or Upper Bavaria is an unforgettable scene; Shrove Tuesday in the Lake Constance region has unmistakable features. At the most beautiful points of this first "flight of stairs", formed by Black Forest, Swabian Alps and Bavarian Alpine foothills, the old architects built the finest Baroque churches — Birnau, Weingarten, In der Wies, or Beuron for instance. In the valleys of the Danube, Lech, Isar, and Inn, however, lying before the next "flight of stairs" formed by the hills of the Palatinate, Spessart, Odenwald and Franconian Jura, grew up the historical old towns of Ulm, Augsburg, Munich, Regensburg — and Passau, with its southern air, at the junction of the Ilz, Inn and Danube. For the most part they were fortunate towns. Trade brought along prosperity and good civic sense or benevolent princes used this wealth for the noble end of furthering culture. Cathedrals, houses of nobles and of wealthy citizens, magnificent secular buildings and parks are to be found here; the table is richly laid with well-spiced food and wines and life often bears a direct, racy character. The farther north one goes, the greater the refinement, though the original core is never entirely lost. The Main has been rightly termed the boundary of the south.

The triangle formed by Rhine, Danube, and Main is considered to be the treasure-house of the south. Even the larger towns such as Heidelberg, Freiburg, Bamberg and incomparable Würzburg have their self-drawn boundaries and are imbued with individuality and intimacy. Perhaps in no other place is such fullness and complete mastery of form to be found among German architects. Dazzling proof of this can be seen particularly in the small towns: Rothenburg, Dinkelsbühl, Nördlingen, Miltenberg, Schwäbisch Hall and Gmünd. One could wander for weeks up and down this part of the country without ever tiring of this feast for the eye. A sail down the Main, say from Vierzehnheiligen, reveals a romantic, fairytale world.

And now the mountains taper down still more — Eifel, Siebengebirge, Westerwald, Taunus, Vogelsberg and Rhön, the last "stair" but one — and rivers herald the plain. The Rhine becomes a mighty torrent attracting our attention. It flows through the lovely Rheingau, where the finest wines mature and cuts its way through the mountains, collecting the waters of the Neckar, Main, Moselle, and Lahn, before heading for ancient Cologne and gay Düsseldorf and the plain of the Lower Rhine. The Weser flows parallel to the Rhine, its banks being lined with attractive little towns strongly imprinted with the North German character, which finally comes into its own behind the last mountain "threshold", the Sauerland, Teutoburger Forest, Weser mountains, Solling and Harz. East of the Weser and west — as far as Soest — the towns of Hildesheim, Brunswick, Celle, and Goslar still bear witness to a proud past.

In the west, the Ruhr district pulsates with new life. Here industry leaves its mark on the landscape. Here in town after town, the glow of blast furnaces lights up the night sky. Here the dark treasures of the earth are brought to light and here lies a great proportion of the nation's wealth. North of Münster, one of the most venerable old towns, the plain begins, stretching as far as the Hanse towns of Bremen, Lübeck and Hamburg, the gateway to the ocean. Schleswig-Holstein juts out beyond the coastline of the North Sea and Baltic, a proud, unyielding, wind-swept land governed by the ebb and flow of the tide. The sea is a wide, rich border.

And now to central Germany. Although scenically it may lack the heroic character of the south it has a charm all of its own: of moderation and intimacy. The softness and harmony of these fir-clad slopes and green valleys rejoice the heart. It is no chance that the noblest minstrels competed on the Wartburg for the laurels of victory; that Luther struggled for expression; that Schiller, the restless Swabian, found peace here and that Goethe, the Frankfurter, made Weimar his adopted home. And when we mention Leipzig and Eisenach, doesn't *Bach*, the name of Germany's greatest musical genius ring in our ears like a fugue? The Harz mountains around the Brocken, the scene of the Witches' Sabbath, might be termed the sister of the "manly" Thuringian Forest. Here was the junction of the medieval highways: it was here that a prince out hunting might hear of his election as King of Germany. These woods are shrouded in a discreet but unmistakable poetry. We have only to look at "Faust" and the "Journey through the Harz". Fertile land lies between these uplands: the "Golden Mead", mythical burial-ground of Barbarossa.

"Saxon Switzerland" is on a grander scale, but despite a modest resemblance to its more imposing namesake, there is no denying its central German character. Anyone who has wandered along the banks of the River Saale knows that apart from the "castles proud and bold", the charm of this part of the country lies in the river meandering past beautiful towns such as Saalfeld, Rudolstadt, Jena, and Naumburg.

Following the course of the Elbe from Wittenberg past Magdeburg and Tangermünde to Wittenberge — the shortest way northwards to the coast —, you will find calm Mecklenburg stretching out as far as the Oder, with Schwerin, Wismar, Rostock, Stralsund and Greifswald, crossed by small lakes and streams. The Mecklenburg lakes are a paradise for fishermen, sparsely populated and therefore all the quieter and more soothing to those in need of a holiday, imbued with a charm all of their own.

The March of Brandenburg with the River Havel and its many lakes, and Frederick the Great's Potsdam, too, form part of the centre: and is there a single Berliner who doesn't appreciate the benefits of this barren land stretching up to the Oder and down to the enchanted stillness of the Spreewald? Today that is all "frontier land" and the sluggish Oder and, beyond Fürstenberg, its tributary the Neisse are "frontier rivers". Let us pause to look over the border at those provinces in which the German feels as completely at home as a Hessian in Hesse, or a Swabian in Swabia. Breslau, hospitable and decorative, is to the Silesian what royal Dresden and "Little Paris" (Leipzig) are to the Saxon. The Silesians are a people of strong emotions, silent, mystic. Industry never got the upper hand in this country, turning its face towards the hills: the Riesengebirge, Eulengebirge, Waldenburger and Glatzer uplands. The Oder was the Silesian's gateway to the world.

It was harder for the Pomeranians, scattered up and down the country. With the exception of Stettin on the western flank and rich, splendid Danzig that didn't strictly belong to Pomerania, there were scarcely any sizeable towns up there. It was farming land with a 190 mile coastline, harbourless except for the old stronghold of Kolberg, but with beautiful forests and fertile soil.

From Pomerania, the road led to East Prussia in closed railway carriages, through the Polish corridor. The East Prussian, like the Silesian, held an outpost; somewhat soberer, more realistic in character than the Silesian, he was no less reliable. Broad as his dialect, he attacked the soil — fertile in the north, but in the southern part, Masuren, marshy and interspersed with lakes and forests; and in the north lay dreaming the Rominter Heide. A rough, beautiful land, loved with an inarticulate love, not unmixed with a little popular self-irony; far from the centre of the Reich, but nevertheless, with its attractive capital Königsberg, birthplace of Kant, an integral part. The E. Prussian coast, with the two great lagoons, the Frische Haff and the Kurische Haff, seems to merge into the sea, a coast of Japanese austerity, a paradise for bird and beast.

The things we build with our hands can mean very much to every one of us, but they are destructible. A landscape, however, escapes the destructive hand of men. Its character, air, its magic, remain intact. The Masuren lakes or the Silesian hills cannot be subdued, the hills of the Harz and the Thuringian Forest cannot be razed, and even if the power to do so lay in the hands of men, the memory we keep in our hearts is unassailable and indestructible.

All this is Germany; we cannot escape the fact. The Germans of to-day are the citizens of a partitioned country, but still children of Germany, an entity. It is the country of their birth, it may be the land for which they yearn. Here, at the end of this survey, it is fitting that we should evoke the name of the sorely-tried capital. For the fate of Germany is reflected in miniature in the fate of Berlin, and Berlin's struggle to regain her freedom and her longing for unity should serve as an example.

The burden of everyday cares and the unpropitious political scene often take our minds off Germany and her capital as an entity. And so in this volume, the separate halves have been united — an event to which Germans look forward with hope, faith, and love.

Rudolf Hagelstange

Schneiders

Beginn einer Deutschlandreise in Bildern: blaue Berge der Alpen, grüne Matten und Kirchen mit Zwiebeltürmen ... St. Koloman bei Füssen.

Starting out on a pictorial trip through Germany: Alpine mountains, green meadows, and impressive churches ... St. Koloman's near Füssen.

1 Départ pour un tour d'Allemagne en photos: montagnes bleuâtres, prés verdoyants, églises de forme caractéristique ... St Koloman près de Füssen.

Baumann

Blaugrüner See unter schneebedeckten Felswänden: der Königssee bei Berchtesgaden mit der Watzmann-Ostwand.

The blue-green waters of the Königssee (near Berchtesgaden) lying beneath the snow-capped crags of the Watzmann.

Un lac bleu-vert que domine une montagne escarpée couverte de neige: le Königssee près de Berchtesgaden avec la face orientale du Watzmann.

Metz

Mit Berchtesgaden unter dem Watzmann beginnt im Südosten das deutsche Bundesgebiet.

Berchtesgaden lies at the foot of the Watzmann, right in the south-east corner of Germany.

Berchtesgaden se niche au pied du Watzmann à l'extrémité sud-est de l'Allemagne.

E. Müller

Der Chiemsee mit der Insel Frauenwörth und den Alpengipfeln,
vom Friedhof in Gstad aus gesehen.

Chiemsee is one of the best-known Bavarian lakes.
The peaceful island of Frauenwörth seen from Gstad cemetery.

Chiemsee, un lac très connu de la Bavière.
L'île tranquille de Frauenwörth, vue du cimétière de Gstad.

Reit im Winkl, ein besonders schneesicheres Skiparadies.

Reit im Winkl, a paradise for skiers.

Reit im Winkl, véritable paradis de neige pour les skieurs.

Zeitz

Neuschwanstein,
auf schroffem Fels
bei Füssen errichtet,
ein steingewordener
königlicher Traum
vom Mittelalter.

Dramatically
perched on a steep crag
near Füssen,
Neuschwanstein
is a nineteenth century
realisation
of a fairy-tale castle.

Neuschwanstein,
qui se dresse
sur un rocher escarpé,
est un château de fées
construit
au dix-neuvième siècle.

Arnold →

Metz

Der Tegernsee mit dem zum Königsschloß ausgebauten alten Kloster.

The Tegernsee and its royal castle, formerly a monastery.

Le lac de Tegernsee avec son château royal, ancien monastère.

Beckert

Partenkirchen, überragt vom Wettersteinmassiv. Die Zugspitze (rechts) ist Deutschlands höchster Gipfel.

Partenkirchen, lying beneath the impressive Wetterstein crag. The Zugspitze (right) is the highest peak in Germany.

Le massif impressionnant du Wetterstein surplombe Partenkirchen. Le Zugspitze (à droite) est le pic le plus haut de l'Allemagne.

Beckert

Die Alpspitze bei Garmisch-Partenkirchen.

The Alpspitze near Garmisch-Partenkirchen.

L'Alpspitze près de Garmisch-Partenkirchen.

Metz

Oberstdorf liegt zu Füßen der mächtigen Allgäuer Berge mit dem Kratzer.

Oberstdorf lies at the foot of the impressive Allgäu mountains. In the background: the Kratzer.

Oberstdorf se niche au pied des montagnes impressionnantes de l'Allgäu. Au fond: le Kratzer.

Einödsbach
im Allgäu
(mit der
Trettachspitze),
der südlichste
bewohnte Punkt
Deutschlands.

Einödsbach
in the Allgäu,
the southernmost
inhabited point
of Germany.
In the background:
the Trettachspitze.

Einödsbach
en Allgäu
à l'extrémité
ud de l'Allemagne.
Au fond:
le Trettachspitze.

Heimhuber

Angermayer

→

Über dem Kirchlein von Steinkirchen am Samerberg
steht feierlich das Licht des Frühlingsmorgens.

The little church of Steinkirchen on the Samerberg invested
with a solemn splendour by the feeble rays of the morning sun.

Le pâle soleil de printemps darde ses premiers rayons
sur la petite église de Steinkirchen dressée sur le Samerberg.

Die spätbarocke Wallfahrtskirche „In der Wies" bei Steingaden
ist ein Höhepunkt abendländischer Baukunst.

The small church "In der Wies" near Steingaden
is a crowning point of occidental architecture.

La petite église «In der Wies» près de Steingaden
représente l'architecture occidentale à son apogée.

13

The spirit
of modern Munich
is to be seen
in the juxtaposition
of this old tower
and the impressive block
of offices
built over the ruins
of the Maxburg
(destroyed 1944).

La maison de commerce
impressionnante
construite pour remplacer
le vieux
château de Maxburg
détruit en 1944
(dont il reste
encore une tour)
représente bien l'esprit
de Munich moderne.

Busch

Das großstädtische Geschäftshaus an der Stelle der 1944 zerstörten Maxburg repräsentiert
mit dem erhalten gebliebenen alten Turm zusammen besonders charakteristisch das moderne München.

München.
Das Neue Rathaus
am Marienplatz,
dahinter die
Türme der
Frauenkirche.

Munich.
The New
Townhall
on Marienplatz,
with the towers
of Frauenkirche
behind.

Munich.
Marienplatz
avec le Nouvel
Hôtel de Ville et,
derrière, les tours
de la Frauenkirche.

Angermayer

Groth-Schmachtenberger

Zu München und Bayern gehört die Geselligkeit beim Bier.

Friendly chat over a stein of beer, a typical Bavarian scene.

Causerie intime dans une brasserie de Munich, scène typique bavaroise.

16

E. Retzlaff

Frische Blumen am Mieder — ein echtes Dirndl.

Fresh flowers on the bodice — a true Dirndl.

Le corsage aux fleurs fraîches fait partie du vrai costume bavarois.

Wasserburg wird vom Inn fast ganz eingeschlossen.

Wasserburg is almost completely encircled by the Inn.

La ville de Wasserburg qu'encercle presque entièrement l'Inn.

Passau. Unterhalb der Feste Oberhaus vereinigen sich die dunklen Wasser der Ilz, die helleren der Donau und die lichten des Inn.

Passau. The dark waters of the Ilz, the grey Danube, and the light-coloured Inn intermingle beneath the fortress of Oberhaus.

Passau. Au pied de la forteresse d'Oberhaus se réunissent les eaux sombres de l'Ilz, les flots gris du Danube et l'eau limpide de l'Inn.

Schmidt-Bavaria

Das Schloß der Grenzstadt Burghausen an der Salzach blickt auf eine lange Geschichte zurück.

Burghausen on the Salzach. Town and castle had a long and varied history.

Burghausen s/Salzach. La ville et le château ont eu une histoire mouvementée.

Wagner

Die alte Bischofsstadt Passau, deren Dom Züge des italienischen Barocks zeigt, hat fast südländischen Charakter.

Passau, an old episcopal town with a cathedral in the Italian manner, shows almost mediterranean traits.

Passau, vieille ville épiscopale avec une cathédrale en baroque italien, a un caractère presque méridional.

Schmidt-Glaßner

Kreuztor und Frauenkirche der alten Residenz Ingolstadt an der Donau.

The Kreuztor and Frauenkirche of the old Bavarian ducal seat of Ingolstadt on the Danube.

La Kreuztor et la Frauenkirche, symboles de la vieille résidence d'Ingolstadt s/Danube.

Schmidt-Glaßner

Der Schimmelturm in Lauingen an der Donau, dem Geburtsort des Albertus Magnus.

The so-called Schimmelturm (White Horse Tower) in Lauingen on the Danube, the birthplace of Albertus Magnus.

La Schimmelturm (tour dite «du Cheval Blanc») à Lauingen s/Danube, lieu de naissance d'Albert le Grand.

Schneiders

Augsburg, die traditionsreiche Hauptstadt Oberschwabens. Blick in die Maximilianstraße, im Hintergrund Rathaus und Dom.

Augsburg, the capital of Upper Swabia, is full of traditions. Our picture: Maximilianstraße with townhall and cathedral as a backdrop.

Augsbourg est la vieille capitale de la Haute Souabe. Maximilianstraße avec, en arrière, l'hôtel de ville et la cathédrale.

24

Busch

Auch im Rathaus von Memmingen zeigt sich die besondere Kunstbegabung der Schwaben.

Memmingen townhall bears witness to the Swabians' remarkable artistic talent.

L'hôtel de ville de Memmingen est témoin du talent artistique des Souabes.

Das Ulmer Münster
besitzt den höchsten
steingemauerten Turm
der Welt (161 m).

The spire of Ulm
cathedral is the
highest masonry
structure
in the world (528 ft).

La flèche de la
cathédrale d'Ulm
(161 m).

Regensburg,
das gotische Portal
des Domes,
altehrwürdig
Donaustadt

Venerable Regensburg
on the Danube.
The Gothic portal
of the cathedral.

La vénérable ville
Ratisbonne s/Danube.
portail gothique
de la cathédrale

Windstoßer 26

Schmidt-Glaßner

Saebens →

Die Klosterkirche von Ottobeuren — eine Krone der Barockarchitektur.

Ottobeuren monastery, a gem of Baroque architecture.

Le monastère d'Ottobeuren, joyau de l'architecture baroque.

Wiblingen bei Ulm. Der barocke Bibliotheksraum des Klosters sucht seinesgleichen.

Wiblingen near Ulm. The Baroque library of the monastery is unparalleled.

Wiblingen près d'Ulm. La bibliothèque baroque du monastère est sans pareil.

Saebens

Das gotische Rathaus des Schwabenstädtchens Waldsee (1426).

The Gothic townhall of the little Swabian town of Waldsee (1426).

L'hôtel de ville gothique du petit bourg souabe de Waldsee (1426).

Aufsberg

Der typisch schwäbische Marktplatz zu Biberach.

The typically Swabian market place of Biberach.

La place du marché typiquement souabe de Biberach.

Windstoßer

32

Ott

←

Bei Burg Werenwag. Der Durchbruch der Oberen Donau durch den Schwäbischen Jura.

Near Werenwag castle. The Upper Danube has cut this gorge through the Swabian Jura.

Gorge aux environs de Werenwag. Le Haut Danube se fraye un chemin à travers le Jura de Souabe.

Hegaulandschaft mit dem Hohentwiel und Singen.

Landscape of Hegau with Hohentwiel and Singen.

Le paysage d'Hegau avec Hohentwiel et Singen.

Lindau: am Hafen der zu Bayern gehörenden Ferieninsel im Schwäbischen Meer, dem Bodensee.

The Bavarian port of Lindau in Lake Constance.

Le port bavarois de Lindau (lac de Constance).

Lauterwasser

Das alte Konstanz am Bodensee und sein Wahrzeichen, der Münsterturm.

The ancient town of Constance with its landmark, the cathedral tower.

La vieille ville de Constance et sa cathédrale.

Lauterwasser

Auf der Meersburg, wo sie sich gern aufhielt, starb die Dichterin Annette von Droste-Hülshoff.

The poetess Annette von Droste-Hülshoff died in Meersburg castle where she had passed part of her life.

Au château de Meersburg vécut et mourut la poétesse Annette von Droste-Hülshoff.

Schneiders

Herbstnachmittag an der Halbinsel von Wasserburg. Zauberhaft ist das ständig wechselnde Spiel des Lichts auf dem Bodensee.

Magical, everchanging interplay of light and shade on Lake Constance: Autumn afternoon on the peninsula of Wasserburg.

Après-midi d'automne sur la presqu'île de Wasserburg. Le jeu toujours changeant de la lumière dans les eaux du lac de Constance est un enchantement.

Schneiders

Eine Zierde des Schwarzwalds sind die mächtigen, mit Holzschindeln gedeckten alemannischen Bauernhäuser.

These sturdy farm houses covered with shingle are the pride of the Black Forest.

Les grosses et solides fermes alemaniques sont, avec leur couverture de bardeaux, une parure de la Forêt Noire.

Saebens

Schwarzwaldtannen bei Baden-Baden.
Black Forest fir-trees near Baden-Baden.
Sapins de la Forêt Noire près de Baden-Baden.

Im Münster
zu Breisach
am Oberrhein
steht einer
der edelsten
spätgotischen
Schreinaltäre.

Beautiful late
Gothic shrine
in Breisach
cathedral on
Upper Rhine.

Belle châsse
datant
des dernières
années
de l'époque
gothique
dans la
cathédrale
de Breisach.

Schneiders

Der Münsterturm der Universitätsstadt Freiburg im Breisgau gilt als der schönste hochgotische Kirchturm.

The spire of the university town of Freiburg is considered one of the most beautiful High Gothic church towers.

La flèche de la cathédrale de Fribourg en Brisgau est parmi les plus belles de l'époque gothique.

Tschira

Das Weltbad Baden-Baden ist seit der Zeit Bismarcks einer der elegantesten Kur- und Erholungsplätze.

The cosmopolitan resort of Baden-Baden has been famous since the age of Bismarck.

La station thermale cosmopolite de Baden-Baden a été célèbre depuis le temps de Bismarck.

Fehr-Bechtel

Karlsruhe, die frühere Hauptstadt des Großherzogtums Baden, ist die Pforte zum Schwarzwald. Das klassizistische Rathaus.

Carlsruhe, the former capital of the grand-duchy of Baden, is the gateway to the Black Forest. The townhall in classical style.

Carlsruhe, ancienne capitale du grand-duché de Bade, est un point de départ pour visiter la Forêt Noire. L'hôtel de ville classique.

R. Müller

Das Zollernschloß Haigerloch an der Eyach in der Schwäbischen Alb.

The castle of Haigerloch on the Eyach in the Swabian Jura.

Le château d'Haigerloch qui domine l'Eyach dans le Jura de Souabe.

Kleinfeld

Tübingen am Neckar: Hölderlinsturm, Alte Aula der Universität und Turm der Stiftskirche.

In the old university town of Tübingen on the Neckar.

Coin de la vieille ville universitaire de Tubingue s/Neckar

Holtmann

Viele Burgen grüßen vom Rande der Schwäbischen Alb weithin ins fruchtbare Unterland. Der Hohenzollern bei Hechingen.

Hohenzollern near Hechingen is one of the many old castles dominating the plain of the Neckar from the edge of the Swabian Jura.

Hohenzollern, près d'Hechingen, est un des nombreux vieux châteaux qui dominent la plaine du Neckar, dressés sur la crête du Jura de Souabe.

Aufsberg

Wie eine feste Burg Gottes ragt das Kloster Groß-Comburg bei Schwäbisch-Hall über die liebliche Kocherlandschaft.

The Benedictine monastery of Gross-Comburg near Schwäbisch-Hall overlooking the lovely valley of the Kocher.

Le monastère Bénédictin de Gross-Comburg près de Schwäbisch-Hall qui commande la belle vallée du Kocher.

Schwäbisch-Gmünd unter dem Rechberg, türmereiche alte Stadt der Goldschmiede.

Many-towered Schwäbisch-Gmünd lying beneath the Rechberg is an old town of goldsmiths.

Schwäbisch-Gmünd, vieille ville d'orfèvres, dresse ses tours nombreuses contre le ciel.

Metz

Metz

Besigheim an der Enz bietet noch heute ein durchaus mittelalterliches Stadtbild.

Besigheim on the Enz, an untouched medieval town.

Besigheim s/Enz, ville médiévale encore intacte.

Das moderne Stuttgart, Baden-Württembergs Hauptstadt, zeigt sich noch immer am wirkungsvollsten in seinem mächtigen Bahnhofsbau von 1927.

Modern Stuttgart, capital of Baden-Württemberg, can be seen most effectively in the massive structure of the railway station (1927).

C'est la gare impressionnante de Stuttgart (1927), capitale de Bade-Wurtemberg, qui révèle le mieux le caractère de la ville moderne.

Das alte Stuttgart verkörpert sich am schönsten in dem prächtigen Arkadenhof des Herzogsschlosses aus der Renaissancezeit.

Old Stuttgart can best be seen in the magnificent arcades of the Renaissance courtyard at the ducal palace.

Ce sont les arcades magnifiques de la cour Renaissance du palais ducal qui incarnent le mieux le vieux Stuttgart.

Holtmann

Markgröningen: das altschwäbische Rathaus während des traditionellen Schäferlaufs.

Markgröningen: the old Swabian townhall during the traditional "Shepherds' Race".

Markgröningen: l'hôtel de ville pendant les fêtes de la « Course des Bergers ».

Saebens

Maulbronn: die Brunnenkapelle dieser besterhaltenen Klosteranlage des hohen Mittelalters in Deutschland.

Maulbronn: the fountain inside the best preserved monastery of the Middle Ages in Germany.

Maulbronn: la fontaine à l'intérieur du monastère médiéval le mieux conservé de l'Allemagne.

Schneiders

Blick vom Fürstenschloß Langenburg a. d. Jagst in das Hohenloher Land.

View from the ducal palace of Langenburg on the Jagst toward the Hohenlohe countryside.

Du château ducal de Langenburg s/Jagst on a une vue étendue du pays de Hohenlohe.

54

Busch

Hirschhorn ist von besonders anmutigem Reiz unter den alten Städtchen am Neckar.

Hirschhorn, an old township on the Neckar, has a charm all of its own.

Parmi les anciennes bourgades qui bordent le Neckar, Hirschhorn se distingue par sa grâce souriante.

Lossen

Neckarlandschaft bei Zwingenberg.

Typical Neckar landscape near Zwingenberg.

Paysage typique du Neckar près de Zwingenberg.

Lossen

Heidelberg, einst die Residenz der Pfalz und älteste deutsche Universität (1386),
ist noch heute ein Zentrum europäischen Geisteslebens und deutscher Studentenromantik.

Heidelberg, former seat of the Electors Palatine, famous for the student-life
of its university, founded in 1386, the oldest in Germany, is still to this day a great centre of learning.

Heidelberg, ancienne résidence des Electeurs Palatins, célèbre par la vie étudiante
de son université fondée en 1386 (la plus ancienne de l'Allemagne), est encore aujourd'hui un centre intellectuel de grande envergure.

Schmidt-Glaßne

Die wuchtige Krypta des Salierdoms zu Speyer birgt das Grabmal Rudolfs von Habsburg.

The proud cathedral of Spires contains in its crypt the tomb of Rudolph of Hapsburg.

Le tombeau de Rodolphe d'Habsbourg dans la crypte de la cathédrale de Spire.

Busch

Worms: der plastisch geformte Dom ist eine Schöpfung aus der Zeit der Staufenka...

Worms cathedral, dating from the days of the Hohenstaufen empe...

La cathédrale de Worms qui date de l'époque des Hohenstau...

Striemann

In der schönen Pfalz ragen die Ruinen vieler Burgen. Blick vom Lindelbrunn zum **Rödelstein**.

In the beautiful hills of the Palatinate lie many fine old castles. View from the castle of Lindelbrunn towards the Rödelstein.

Maint vieux château domine le joli paysage du Palatinat. Le Rödelstein vu du château de Lindelbrunn.

Die große Saarschleife bei Mettlach.
The great loop of the River Saar near Mettlach.
La grande boucle formée par la Sarre près de Mettlach.

Wantz

Häusser

Die einstige Residenz Mannheim ist heute ein Zentrum der Industrie. – Der Friedrichsplatz.

Mannheim, formerly a ducal seat, is today an industrial centre. Our picture: Friedrichsplatz.

Mannheim, ancienne résidence, est aujourd'hui un centre industriel. Dans la photo: Friedrichsplatz.

Wolff & Tritschler

Schwetzingen: Fontäne im barocken Park des Lustschlosses der Pfälzer Kurfürsten.

Fountain in the Baroque park of Schwetzingen, country seat of the Electors Palatine.

Schwetzingen: fontaine du parc baroque qui entoure le château des Electeurs Palatins.

Wolff & Tritschler

→

Bad Mergentheim. Deutschmeisterbrunnen und Schloß des Deutschen Ordens.

Bad Mergentheim. Deutschmeister fountain and castle of the Teutonic Order.

Bad Mergentheim. Fontaine «Deutschmeister» et château de l'Ordre Teutonique.

Rittersaal in Schloß Weikersheim an der Tauber (1605)

Knights' Hall in Weikersheim on the Tauber (1605)

Salle des Chevaliers, Weikersheim sur la Tauber (1605)

Wolff & Tritschler

Harburg an der Wörnitz beherrscht die „Romantische Straße" von Füssen nach Würzburg, auf der einst der Handel zwischen Süd und Nord seinen Weg nahm.
Harburg castle high above the Wörnitz guards the "Romantic Road", formerly the important north-south trading route from Füssen to Würzburg.
Le château d'Harbourg qui surplombe le Wörnitz veillait autrefois sur l'ancienne route commerciale qui reliait l'Italie et le nord, passant par Füssen et Wurtzbourg.

Nördlingen: das einzigartige Luftbild der alten Reichsstadt an der Romantischen Straße, Mittelpunkt des fruchtbaren schwäbischen Ries.

Nördlingen: bird's eye view of the old free imperial city on the "Romantic Road", centre of the fertile Swabian district of Ries.

Nördlingen: vue aérienne de l'ancienne ville libre souabe, centre du pays fertile du «Ries».

Strähle

Nördlingen: der alte Wehrgang
beim Löpsinger Tor.

Nördlingen: the old ramparts
near the Löpsingen Gate.

Nördlingen: vieux remparts
près de la Porte Löpsingen.

Wolff & Tritschler

→
Nördlingen:
das gotische Rathaus
vom Turm der Stadtkirche
St. Georg aus.

Nördlingen: the Gothic townhall
seen from St. George's.

Nördlingen: l'hôtel de ville
gothique vu de l'église
St. Georges.

E. Retzlaff

E. Retzlaff

Schwäbischer Schäfer aus dem Ries.

Shepherd from the Ries district of Swabia.

Pasteur souabe du pays de Ries.

E. Retzlaff

Fränkische Bäuerin aus Effeltrich.
Franconian country woman from Effeltrich.
Paysanne franconienne d'Effeltrich.

E. Hase

Das Ellinger Tor im fränkischen Weissenburg.

The Ellingen Gate in the Franconian town of Weissenburg.

La Porte d'Ellingen dans la ville franconienne de Weissenburg.

Das Herz Frankens, dieses Inbegriffs deutscher Romantik, ist Rothenburg ob der Tauber. — Röderbogen und Markusturm.

Rothenburg on the Tauber, the heart of Franconia, is the epitome of German romanticism. Röder Arch and Markus Tower.

La Franconie réunit tous les charmes des sites romantiques de l'Allemagne. Rothenburg s/Tauber en est le cœur. L'arc Röder et la Tour St Marc.

73

Busch

Rothenburg o. d. Tauber: das Spitaltor der alten Reichsstadt.

Rothenburg o. Tauber: the Hospital Gate of the old free imperial city.

Rothenburg s/Tauber: la Porte de l'Hôpital de cette vieille ville libre.

Rothenburg:
die Justitia
am Rathaus.

Rothenburg:
Justice,
figure
at the
townhall.

Rothenburg:
la Justice,
statue
à l'hôtel
de ville.

Busch

75

Rothenburg o. d. Tauber. Das Plönlein bietet einen Blick auf zwei Stadttore.

One of the loveliest sights of Rothenburg: the Plönlein, with a view toward two of the old city gates.

Une des parties des plus pittoresques de Rothenburg: le Plönlein avec deux des vieilles portes de la ville.

Aufsberg

Aus dem alten Reichsstädtchen Dinkelsbühl; Rothenburger Tor und Spital.

The Rothenburg Gate and hospital in the old free imperial city of Dinkelsbühl.

La porte Rothenburg et l'hôpital de la vieille ville libre de Dinkelsbühl.

St. Georg in Dinkelsbühl (1448-92),
der einheitlich reifste
aller Hallenkirchbauten
in Süddeutschland.

St. George's in Dinkelsbühl
(1448-92)
is the most mature of all church
buildings of its type
in S. Germany.

L'église St. Georges
à Dinkelsbühl (1448-92) dépasse
en hardiesse de conception tous
les édifices de son genre dans le
Sud de l'Allemagne.

→

Eichstätt in Franken:
das Mortuarium
des Domes (1484).

Eichstätt in Franconia:
the mortuary chapel
in the cathedral (1484).

Eichstätt en Franconie:
chapelle mortuaire
de la cathédrale (1484).

Busch

Nürnberg. Blick von der Burg auf Dürers Wohnhaus am Thiergärtner Tor.

Nuremberg: view of Dürer's house at the Thiergärtner Gate, seen from the castle.

Nuremberg: la maison de Dürer près de la Porte Thiergärtner, vue du château.

Busch

Nürnberg: der Blick aus Albrecht Dürers Arbeitszimmer auf den Sinwellturm der Burg, das Wahrzeichen der Stadt.
Nuremberg: view from Albrecht Dürer's study window onto the Sinwell Tower of the castle, a landmark of Nuremberg.
Nuremberg: la Tour Sinwell, symbole de Nuremberg, vue du cabinet de travail d'Albrecht Dürer.

1

Busch

Ansbach in Mittelfranken. Markgrafenschloß.

Ansbach in Central Franconia: the Margraves' castle.

Ansbach dans la Moyenne-Franconie: le château des Margraves.

Gundermann

Bayreuth in Oberfranken, die Stadt Richard Wagners, besitzt auch das besterhaltene Barocktheater.

Bayreuth in Upper Franconia, famous for its Wagner Festival, has the best preserved Baroque theatre in Germany.

Bayreuth dans la Haute-Franconie, célèbre par son Festival Richard Wagner, possède le théâtre baroque le mieux conservé de l'Allemagne.

In der „Fränkischen Schweiz".

In "Franconian Switzerland".

« La Suisse Franconienne ».

Die Wallfahrtskirche Vierzehnheiligen ist das Kleinod des fränkischen Barocks.

The pilgrimage church of the Vierzehnheiligen is the gem of Franconian Baroque art.

Le pélérinage des Vierzehnheiligen est le joyau de l'art baroque franconien.

Schmidt-Glaßner ⟶

Plösser   84

Wolff
& Tritschler

Bamberg: über der alten Bischofsstadt ragt der mächtige Dom aus der Zeit der Staufer.

Bamberg: the magnificent cathedral, dating back to the Hohenstaufen days, rises above the old episcopal seat of Bamberg.

Bamberg: la cathédrale magnifique datant de la période Hohenstaufen domine la vieille ville épiscopale de Bamberg.

Der Bamberger Dom
birgt eine Fülle deutscher
Plastik, darunter den
„Bamberger Reiter"
(um 1235),
das Sinnbild christlich-
abendländischen
Rittertums.

In Bamberg cathedral
a wealth of classical
German sculpture can
be seen, among them the
"Bamberg Knight"
(ca. 1235),
symbol of Christian
chivalry.

La cathédrale de Bamberg
est riche en sculptures
allemandes, dont le
«Chevalier de Bamberg»,
symbole de la chevalerie
chrétienne.

Hege

Metz

Marktbreit, eines der vielen altfränkischen Städtchen am Main.

Marktbreit, one of the many old Franconian townships on the Main.

Marktbreit, un des nombreux bourgs franconiens situés le long du Mein.

aebens

Die Fürstbischöfe von Würzburg, zugleich Herzoge in Franken, besaßen in der Feste Marienberg das wichtigste Bollwerk über dem alten Mainübergang.

The fortress of Marienberg, a mighty bastion at the Main crossing, was the seat of the Prince-Bishops of Würzburg.

Le vaste bastion de Marienberg qui garde le passage du Mein fut la résidence des Princes-Evêques de Wurtzbourg.

Schloßverwaltung

Weissenstein ob Pommersfelden: das großartige Treppenhaus des bischöflichen Schlosses, des ersten der großen Barockschlösser in Deutschland (1711-18).

Weissenstein ob Pommersfelden: the magnificent staircase in the episcopal palace, the first of the great Baroque palaces in Germany.

Weissenstein ob Pommersfelden: l'escalier magnifique du palais épiscopal, le premier des grands palais baroques en Allemagne.

Saebens

Die Gartenfront der Würzburger Residenz (1719–50), deren Treppenhaus ebenso berühmt ist wie das in Pommersfelden und das in Brühl.

Würzburg Palace, the facade overlooking the park. No less famous than the staircases at Pommersfelden and Brühl is the one at Würzburg.

Palais de Wurtzbourg: façade donnant sur le parc. L'escalier du palais est aussi renommé que ceux de Pommersfelden et de Brühl.

Busch

← Wolff & Tritschler

Das Rathaus von Michelstadt im Odenwald (1484).

The townhall of Michelstadt in the Odenwald (1484).

L'hôtel de ville de Michelstadt en Odenwald (1484).

Miltenberg am Main. Reiches fränkisches Fachwerk am „Schnatterloch".

Miltenberg on the Main. Fine specimens of Franconian half-timbering on the market place.

De belles maisons à colombage franconiennes, donnant sur la place du marché de Miltenberg.

Mespelbrunn,
ein versteckt liegendes
Wasserschlößchen im Spessart.

Mespelbrunn, a moated castle
tucked away in the depths
of the Spessart.

Le château de Mespelbrunn,
entouré d'un lac,
se perd parmi
les forêts du Spessart.

← Göllner

Busch

Darmstadt: Blick vom Schloß auf Stadtkirche und Rathaus der ehemaligen Residenzs
Darmstadt, a former ducal seat: view of the town church and townhall seen from the ca
Darmstadt, ancienne résidence ducale; l'église et l'hôtel de ville vus du châ

Falke

Das alte und das neue Frankfurt: beim Eschenheimer Turm.

Frankfort old and new: near the Eschenheimer Tower.

Le Francfort d'autrefois et celui d'aujourd'hui: environs de la Tour Eschenheim.

Wolff & Tritschler

Frankfurt a. M.: im Goethehau

Frankfort on the M

Francfort s/Mein: l'inte

Göllner

Das Kurhaus in Wiesbaden, der Landeshauptstadt Hessens.

Wiesbaden (capital of Hesse), the Kurhaus.

Wiesbaden (capitale de l'Hesse): le casino.

Busch

Der Brunnenhof in Bad Nauheim, dem Herzbad am Taunus.

The Brunnenhof (Fountain Court) in Bad Nauheim, a spa near the Taunus much frequented by sufferers from heart disease.

99 La Brunnenhof (Cour de la Fontaine) de Bad Nauheim, station thermale située près des montagnes du Taunus, qui attire beaucoup de malades souffrant du cœur.

Jeiter

Blick auf Fulda mit Michaelskapelle und Bonifatius-Dom.

View of Fulda showing the St. Michael's chapel and the cathedral.

Fulda: la chapelle St Michael et la cathédrale.

H. Retzlaff

Bad Hersfeld: das bedeutende Baudenkmal der 1760 zerstörten Ottonischen Stiftskirche.

Bad Hersfeld: the impressive collegiate church, destroyed in 1760.

Bad Hersfeld: l'église collégiale, monument important détruit en 1760.

Dorf Habel in der Rhön, ein rechtes Stück deutscher Heimat.

The village of Habel in the Rhön mountains.

Le village d'Habel situé dans les montagnes du Rhön.

Ebert

Kassel: Blick vom „Herkules" auf Schloß Wilhelmshöhe und die Stadt.

Kassel: town and castle seen from the "Hercules".

Cassel: la ville dominée par le château de Wilhelmshöhe.

Der Marktplatz von Butzbach in der Wetterau. Das hübsche Rathaus besaß ursprünglich eine offene Bogenhalle.

Butzbach market place and townhall (originally with portico).

Butzbach: la place du marché et l'hôtel de ville (originellement à portique).

Busc

104

Melsungen in Hessen. Selten findet man noch ein so rein erhaltenes Bild einer ländlichen Kleinstadt.

Melsungen in Hesse, an exceptionally well-preserved old town.

Melsungen en Hesse, vieille ville dans un état de conservation excellent.

105

Eine romantische Idylle:
Das alte Solms'sche Schloß in Hungen
am Vogelsberg.

The romantic castle of Hungen,
home of the Counts of Solms,
on the edge of the Vogelsberg.

Hungen près du Vogelsberg:
le château romantique des comtes de Solms.

Busch   **106**

Busch

Schmuck wie Hessens bunte Volkstrachten sind seine freundlichen Fachwerkbauten. — Rathaus auf dem Marktplatz zu Alsfeld.
Hesse's cheery half-timbered buildings are as trim and neat as the colourful regional costumes. Townhall of Alsfeld.
Comme ses habitants avec leurs costumes traditionnels, la Hesse se pare aimablement de maisons à colombage. Alsfeld: l'hôtel de ville.

Die schönen bunten Hessentrachten in der Gegend von Marburg sind wie die in der Schwalm (unser Bild) noch nicht ganz ausgestorben.

The brightly coloured regional dress of Hesse has not yet died out. Peasant girls in the Schwalm district.

Le beau costume multicolore de pays d'Hesse se porte encore dans quelques régions, dans celle de Schwalm par exemple.

Saebens

Ruine Vetzberg im großen Lahnknie bei Gießen (von der Ruine Gleiberg aus).

The ruined castle of Vetzberg, at the river bend near Giessen (seen from the Gleiberg).

Le château en ruines de Vetzberg où la Lahn fait un grand coude près de Giessen (vu du Gleiberg).

Marburg. In der Grabeskirche der hl. Elisabeth ruhen die Landgrafen von Hessen wie auch Reichspräsident v. Hindenburg.

Marburg. The landgraves of Hesse were buried in St. Elisabeth's church which also contains the remains of President v. Hindenburg.

Marburg. Les vieux landgraves de Hesse furent enterrés dans l'église Ste Elisabeth, ainsi que le Président v. Hindenburg.

110

Marburg an der Lahn.
Das Landgrafenschloß
krönt das Gassengewirr
der Universitätsstadt.

The castle of the
landgraves commands
a good view of the
tangled streets in the
university town of
Marburg on the Lahn.

Marburg. Le château des
landgraves domine les
vieilles rues de cette
ville universitaire.

Busch

Schloß Runkel an der Lahn, eine eindrucksvolle Burgruine aus romanischer Zeit.

Runkel castle on the Lahn, an impressive ruin in Romanesque style.

Le château de Runkel sur la Lahn, ruine majestueuse, construit dans le style roman.

Busch

112

Busch

Limburg. Der Dom St. Georg über der Lahn ist ein spätes Meisterwerk aus der alten deutschen Kaiserzeit (1235).

Limburg. St. George's cathedral overlooking the Lahn is an architectural masterpiece (1235).

Limburg. La cathédrale St Georges qui domine la Lahn est un chef-d'œuvre datant du temps des Empereurs germaniques (1235).

Busch

Der Dom im „Goldenen Mainz" ist der glanzvollste der drei großen Kaiserdome am Rhein.

The cathedral of "Golden Mainz" ist the most splendid of the three great imperial cathedrals on the Rhine.

La cathédrale de « Mayence la Dorée » est la plus splendide des trois grandes cathédrales impériales du Rhin.

Rotgans

Koblenz. Blick auf das „Deutsche Eck" zwischen Rhein und Mosel von der ehemaligen Festung Ehrenbreitstein aus.

Coblenz. View from Ehrenbreitstein, a former fortress, of the "Deutsche Eck" between the Rhine and the Moselle.

Coblence. Le « Deutsche Eck », triangle formé par le confluent du Rhin et de la Moselle, vu de l'ancienne forteresse d'Ehrenbreitstein.

Wolff & Tritschler

Oberwesel am Rhein mit der Liebfrauenkirche und der Schönburg.

Oberwesel on the Rhine with the Liebfrauenkirche (Church of Our Lady) and the castle of Schönburg.

Oberwesel s/Rhin. La Liebfrauenkirche (Notre Dame) et le château de Schönburg.

Wolff & Tritschler

„Die Katz" am Rhein, Burg Neukatzenelnbogen über St. Goarshausen, liegt St. Goar gegenüber.

Neukatzenelnbogen castle overlooking St. Goarshausen, opposite St. Goar on the Rhine.

Le château de Neukatzenelnbogen, qui domine St Goarshausen, est situé en face de St Goar s/Rhin.

Rotgans

Bei der Lorelei (linker Felsen) erkennt man besonders eindringlich, wie der Rhein seinen Weg in das Schiefergebirge hineingefressen hat.

Near the Lorelei (crag on the left), one is struck by the manner in which the Rhine has eaten its way into the slate mountains.

On est frappé en regardant la manière dont le Rhin s'est frayé un chemin à travers les montagnes d'ardoise près du Lorelei (rocher à gauche)

Jeiter

Zell an der Mosel, der kleineren Schwester des Rheins.
Zell is situated on the River Moselle, smaller sister of the Rhine.
Zell, situé sur la Moselle, petite sœur du Rhin.

Wolff & Tritschler

Die herbe Landschaft der Eifel zeigt noch deutlich den Charakter ihrer vulkanischen Entstehung.

The austere countryside of the Eifel hills plainly shows their volcanic origin.

Les paysages montagneuses de l'Eifel montrent encore leur origine vulcanique.

→

Burg Eltz, zwischen Wäldern tief versteckt,
erhebt sich unweit der Mosel über dem Eltzbach.

Eltz castle hidden away in the forests
overlooks the River Eltzbach near the Moselle.

Le château d'Eltz, perdu parmi des forêts épaisses,
commande la vallée de l'Eltzbach, non loin de la Moselle.

Aachen. In der schon unter Karl d. Großen errichteten Pfalzkapelle, dem Münster, steht der Krönungsstuhl der alten deutschen Könige und Kaiser.

Aix-la-Chapelle. The coronation throne of the German kings and emperors stands in the cathedral founded by Charlemagne.

Aix-la-Chapelle. Le trône qui a servi au couronnement des rois et des empereurs allemands se trouve dans la cathédrale fondée par Charlemagne.

122

Wolff & Tritschler

Darstellung Karls des Großen am Marienschrein in Aachen, einer der bedeutendsten Goldschmiedearbeiten des Mittelalters (um 1220).
Charlemagne as portrayed by medieval goldsmiths on the priceless St. Mary's shrine (ca. 1220) in Aix-la-Chapelle.
Charlemagne, chef-d'œuvre de l'orfèvrerie médiévale ciselé sur la châsse Ste Marie (c. 1220) qui se trouve à Aix-la-Chapelle.

Sander

Das Siebengebirge mit dem Drachenfels und der Wolkenburg; links der Petersberg, vom Rolandsbogen aus gesehen.

The Siebengebirge (Seven Hills) with the Drachenfels and Wolkenburg castle; left: the Petersberg seen from Roland's Bow.

La Siebengebirge, dont le Drachenfels, et le château de Wolkenburg; à gauche: le Petersberg vu du Rolandsbogen (l'Arc de Roland).

Der Rhein, Deutschlands bedeutendster Fluß, entfaltet seinen romantischen Reiz am schönsten zur Zeit der Weinlese. Lorch am Rhein.

The Rhine, Germany's most important river, is most charming at the time of the grape-harvest. Lorch on the Rhine.

Le Rhin, le fleuve le plus important de l'Allemagne, épanouit tout son charme romantique à la saison des vendanges. Lorch sur le Rhin.

Wolff & Tritschler

Claasen

Das Rheinufer in Köln wird von der Silhouette des Doms bestimmt, jenes mächtigen Denkmals spätmittelalterlicher Frömmigkeit.

The silhouette of the cathedral, a monument to medieval piety, overshadows the Rhine bank at Cologne.

A Cologne, la rive du Rhin est dominée par la silhouette de la cathédrale, splendide témoignage de la piété médiévale.

126

Die Universitätsstadt Bonn wurde vorläufige Hauptstadt der Bundesrepublik Deutschland. Der Plenarsaal des Bundeshauses.

The university town of Bonn was made provisional capital of the Federal Republic. Full session of the Federal Diet.

La ville universitaire de Bonn est devenue capitale provisoire de la République Fédérale. Assemblée plénière du parlement.

Hallensleben →

Rheinisches
Museum

Köln. Hochamt im wiederhergestellten Dom (1248–1322, vollendet erst 1880).

Cologne. High mass celebrated in the restored cathedral (1248–1322, completed 1880).

Köln. Ausschnitt aus Stephan Lochners Dombild (um 1440).

Cologne. Stephan Lochner's picture in the cathedral (ca. 1440, detail).

Cologne. La grand'messe célébrée dans la cathédrale restaurée

Cologne. Le tableau de Stephan Lochner (c. 1440, détail) dans la cathédrale.

(1248–1322, terminée en 1880).

128

Siebert

Düsseldorf. Das Alte Rathaus (1573) der eleganten Rheinmetropole mit dem Reiterstandbild des Pfälzer Kurfürsten Jan Wellem (1711).

Düsseldorf. The Old Townhall (1573) of the elegant Rhine metropolis with the equestrian statue of the Elector Palatine Jan Wellem (1711).

Düsseldorf. La statue équestre de l'Electeur Palatin Jan Wellem (1711) devant le Vieil Hôtel de Ville (1573) de l'élégante métropole rhénane.

Strache

Neuß am Rhein, Düsseldorf gegenübergelegen, besitzt den reifsten der rheinischen Dome aus der romanischen Stilepoche (begonnen 1209).

Neuss opposite Düsseldorf boasts the most mature of Rhenish Romanesque cathedrals (begun 1209).

La cathédrale romanesque de Neuss, ville située en face de Dusseldorf, dépasse en hardiesse de conception toutes celles de la Rhénanie.

Saebens

→

Niederrheinisches Gehöft bei Xanten.

Lower Rhine farmhouse near Xanten.

Ferme typique de la Basse-Rhénanie près de Xanten.

Land am Strom. In der Ferne Hamborn.

River landscape. In the distance, Hamborn.

Paysage rhénan près de Hamborn.

Andres

Wichtige Stadt im Ruhrgebiet: Essen, der Bahnhofsplatz.

An important centre in the Ruhr district: Essen, the station square.

Dans les villes de la Ruhr: Essen, place de la gare.

Dortmund. Auch hier, in der größten Stadt Westfalens, baut man großzügig wieder auf.

Dortmund, Westphalia's largest town. Here, too, there is evidence of grand-scale reconstruction.

Dortmund. Ici aussi, dans la plus grande ville de la Westphalie, la réconstruction avance à grands pas.

Binz

Schichtwechsel der „Kumpels" einer Kohlengrube bei Moers.

Coal miners changing shift near Moers.

Changement d'équipe dans une mine de charbon près de Mœrs.

Laboratorium in einem Werk der chemischen Großindustrie.

Laboratory in one of the big chemical works in the Rhineland.

Laboratoire d'une des grandes usines chimiques en Rhénanie.

Hallensleben

←

Das Ruhrgebiet, wie man es sich vorstellt. Kupferhütte und DEMAG in Duisburg.

Popular conception of the Ruhr district — industrial plants in Duisburg.

La Ruhr comme on se la représente toujours: industrie à Duisburg.

Kohle und Benzin auf dem Rhein-Herne-Kanal bei Gelsenkirchen.

Coal and petrol on the Rhine-Herne canal near Gelsenkirchen.

Chalands chargés de charbon et d'essence sur le canal Rhin-Herne.

Das berühmte Rathaus zu Münster (um 1335), in dem 1648 ein Teil des Westfälischen Friedens geschlossen wurde.

Münster's famous townhall (ca. 1335) in which part of the treaty of Westphalia was concluded in 1648.

L'hôtel de ville célèbre de Münster (c. 1335), où fut conclue en 1648 une partie du traité de Westphalie.

Lindemann

Soest. Der Turm des **Patroklusmünsters (um 1100)** ist das eindrucksvollste Zeugnis westfälischer Art.

Soest. The tower of St. Patroklus' Cathedral (ca. 1100) is the most impressive of its kind in Westphalia.

Soest. La flèche de la Cathédrale St Patroklus **(c. 1100) est la plus impressionnante** de toutes celles en son genre en Westphalie.

Strähle

Das westfälische Wasserschloß Gemen bei Borken in Westfalen.

The Westphalian moated castle of Gemen near Borken.

Le château de Gemen près de Borken en Westphalie.

142

Busch

In Westfalen hat sich der Zauber der wehrhaften deutschen Wasserschlösser am besten bewahrt. — Burg Vischering bei Lüdinghausen.

Vischering castle near Lüdinghausen in Westphalia, magic land of well-preserved moated castles.

C'est en Westphalie que s'est le mieux conservé le charme des châteaux-forts entourés de fossés. — Le château de Vischering.

Busch

Unter Buchen und Eichen säumen stolze Höfe in Niedersachsen den sandigen Heideweg. — Hedendorf im Landkreis Stade.

The sandy moorland paths of Lower Saxony are dotted with shady farms. Tree-ringed Hedendorf near Stade.

En Basse Saxe, de belles fermes abritées par des hêtres et des chênes bordent le chemin sableux qui conduit à travers la lande. Hedendorf près de Stade.

Hallensleben

Im schönen Sauerland. Das Weischedetal.

Beautiful Sauerland. The Weischede valley.

La vallée de la Weischede dans la belle région de Sauerland.

E. Retzlaff

Niedersächsischer Bauer aus dem Bückeburger Land.

Lower Saxon farmer from the district of Bückeburg.

Paysan de la Basse-Saxe (des environs de Bückeburg).

Busch

Die Wehlburg (1750) bei Badbergen im Artland ist sicherlich das schönste niederdeutsche Bauernhaus.

The "Wehlburg" (1750) near Badbergen is surely the most beautiful of all Lower Saxon farmhouses.

Le «Wehlburg» (1750) près de Badbergen est certainement la plus belle ferme de la Basse-Saxe.

Osnabrück.
Blick über
die Dächer
auf St. Johannis.

Osnabrück.
View of St. John's
across the roofs.

Osnabrück.
L'église St Jean
domine les toits.

Schneiders

Saebens

Lemgo. Der Marktplatz des alten Hansestädtchens im lippischen Hügelland.

Lemgo. The market place of the old Hanse town in the hilly country of Lippe.

Lemgo. La place du marché de cette vieille ville hanséatique située dans le pays montueux de Lippe.

Wagner

Busch →

Das obere Wesertal bei Steinmühle.

The valley of the upper Weser near Steinmühle.

La vallée de la haute Weser près de Steinmühle.

Schloß Hämelschenburg zeigt die Schmuckfreude des Stiles der sogenannten Weser-Renaissance.

Hämelschenburg castle, a typically ornate product of the "Weser Renaissance".

Le château de Hämelschenburg, riche en ornement, est typique du style «Renaissance Weser».

Hildesheim.
Das unvergessene
Knochenhauer-
Amtshaus (1529).

Hildesheim.
The unforgettable
Knochenhauer-
Amtshaus (1529).

Hildesheim.
Le Knochenhauer-
Amtshaus (1529)
fut totalement détruit.

Der Engelschor
der herrlichen
Michaeliskirche (1033)
in Hildesheim.

The famous
Angels' Choir (1033)
of the Michaeliskirche
(St. Michael's)
at Hildesheim.

Le célèbre chœur (1033)
de la Michaeliskirche
à Hildesheim.

Busch

Sommer und Winter
im waldreichen
Harzgebirge.

Summer and winter
in the wooded
Harz mountains.

Scène d'été et
scène d'hiver
dans les montagnes
boisées du Harz.

155   Rudolphi

Busch

Goslar. Der Reichsadler auf dem alten Marktbrunnen (14. Jahrh.).

Goslar. The imperial eagle on the old fountain of the market place (14th century).

Goslar. L'aigle impérial couronne la vieille fontaine (datant du 14e siècle) au milieu de la place du marché.

156

Hege

Braunschweig. Der Löwe, den sich der stolze Herzog Heinrich von Bayern und Niedersachsen (1129—95) setzen ließ.

Brunswick. The lion set up by proud Duke Henry of Bavaria and Lower Saxony (1129—95).

Brunswick. Le lion érigé par le fier duc Henri de Bavière et de Basse-Saxe (1129—95).

Braunschweig. Der Ostgiebel des Gewandhauses (1591) ist das wichtigste Werk der Renaissance in der Welfenstadt.

Brunswick. The East facade of the Gewandhaus (1591) is the town's foremost Renaissance monument.

Brunswick. La façade orientale du Gewandhaus (1591) est le monument principal du style renaissance dans la ville.

Busch

Goslar. Die prachtvoll erhaltene Ratsstube (um 1520), ein Meisterwerk spätgotischer Raumausstattung.

Goslar. The magnificently preserved council-chamber (ca. 1520), a masterpiece of Late Gothic decoration.

159

Goslar. Le décor magnifique de la salle du conseil (c. 1520) est un chef-d'œuvre datant de la dernière époque de l'art gothique.

Andres

→

Das imposante Neue Rathaus (1900–1913) von Hannover,
Zeugnis der wilhelminischen Epoche.

Hanover: the imposing new city hall (1900–1913)
with an artificial lake in the foreground.

Hanover. Le nouvel hôtel de ville (1900–1913)
et le lac artificiel dans Maschpark.

Hannover. Abendliche Szene in der vorbildlich wiederaufgebauten Innenstadt.

Hanover has been rebuilt as a thoroughly modern city. Street scene at night.

Hanover, ville tout à fait moderne après la reconstruction. Scène de nuit.

Lüden

Straße in Stade.

Street in Stade.

Rue de Stade.

→
Celle.
Buntes
Straßenbild
der alten
Residenzstadt.

In the colourful
old town of Celle.

Coin de la ville
pittoresque
de Celle.

← Saebens →

162

Busch

→

Lüneburg. Die breite Marktstraße „Am Sande" mit der Johanniskirche.

Lüneburg. The Johanniskirche (St. John's) on the wide "Sand", a market street.

Lüneburg. La Johanniskirche (L'église St Jean) qui domine la «Sand», large rue de marché.

Lüneburg. Einer der prachtvollen Backsteingiebel der Hansezeit.

Lüneburg. One of the splendid brick gables to be found in this old Hanse town.

Lüneburg. Un des magnifiques pignons en briques qui caractérisent cette vieille ville hanséatique.

Lüden

Boy-Schmidt

Heidehof Bockheber bei Wilsede.   Im Totengrund der Lüneburger Heide bei Wilsede.

Bockheber Farm on the heath near Wilsede.   The Lüneburg Heath near Wilsede. ''Valley of the Dead''.

La ferme de Bockheber au milieu des landes près de Wilsede.   Les landes de Lunebourg (aux environs de Wilsede). «Vallée des Morts».

Dodenhoff

→

Niederdeutscher Winter im Niederungsgebiet bei Worpswede.

Winter on the plain near Worpswede.

L'hiver sur la plaine près de Worpswede.

Torfkähne auf der Hamme im Teufelsmoor.

Barges loaded with peat sailing down the R. Hamme
through the Teufelsmoor (Devil's bog).

Des chalands chargés de tourbe remontent la Hamme,
en passant par le Teufelsmoor (terrain marécageux).

Saebens

169

Saebens

Niederdeutsches Land. Blick vom Weyerberg bei Worpswede.

N. German landscape. View from the Weyerberg near Worpswede.

Paysage de l'Allemagne du nord, vu du Weyerberg près de Worpswede.

ebens

Deiche schützen das flache deutsche Küstenland im Marschengebiet wie hier an der Unterweser.

The flat German coastal area is protected by dykes. Above: marshy land on the R. Weser.

Le littoral bas de la Mer du Nord est protégé par des digues. Au-dessus: terrain marécageux traversé par la basse Weser.

E. Retzlaff

Fischfang auf hoher See ist harte Arbeit und braucht ganze Kerle.

Deep-sea fishing is rough work and requires tough men.

La pêche au long cours a besoin d'hommes tenaces.

Neuharlingersiel, einer der kleinen Hafenorte zwischen Greetsiel und Dagebüll.

Neuharlingersiel, one of the small coastal harbours between Greetsiel and Dagebüll.

Neuharlingersiel, un des petits ports de pêche entre Greetsiel et Dagebüll.

Das ehrwürdige
Rathaus zu Bremen . . .
. . . und sein
Großer Festsaal.

Bremen townhall . . .
. . . and its great
banqueting hall.

L'hôtel de ville
de Brême . . .
. . . et sa salle
des fêtes.

← Saebens →

Germin

Andres →

Geschäftshäuser der Hamburger Innenstadt.
Blick von der Petrikirche in die Steinstraße.

Hamburgs Alsterseite von der Lombardsbrücke aus.

Hamburg. The Alster side seen from the Lombard Bridge.

Hambourg du côté de l'Alster vu du Pont Lombard.

Office buildings in the city of Hamburg.
View of Steinstrasse seen from St. Peter's.

Maisons de commerce au centre de la ville d'Hambourg.
La Steinstrasse vue de l'église St Pierre.

176

Hamburgs Elbhafen bei der Überseebrücke.

Hamburg. Elbe docks near Überseebrücke.

Hambourg. Le port de l'Elbe près de l'Überseebrücke.

Hamburg-Blankenese. Blick über die breite Niederelbe.
Hamburg-Blankenese. View across the wide lower Elbe.
Hambourg-Blankenese. Panorame de la basse Elbe.

Göllner

Busch

Heißer Tag in der Sandwelt der Nordseedünen.

A hot day on the North Sea sand-dunes.

Jour de chaleur parmi les dunes de la Mer du Nord.

Busch

Abend am Strand.
Evening on the beach.
Soirée sur la plage.

181

Wagne

Sylt. Steilküste am Roten Kliff.

Sylt. At the "Red Cliff".

Sylt. Au «Rote Kliff».

Schensky

Die Nordspitze des Buntsandsteinfelsens Helgoland in der Deutschen Bucht.

The northern tip of Heligoland, a rock of bright red sandstone.

L'extrémité nord d'Helgoland, rocher en grès de couleur rouge.

Friedrichstadt an der Eider, eine niederdeutsche Idylle.

Friedrichstadt on the Eider, a North German idyll.

Friedrichstadt sur l'Eider, idylle au nord de l'Allemagne.

Schneiders

Aus der „Rosenstadt" Eutin inmitten der schönen Holsteinischen Schweiz.

Eutin, "town of roses", lying in the heart of "Holstein Switzerland".

Eutin, «ville des roses», située en pleine «Suisse d'Holstein».

Bauer

Husum. Ein Bild wie aus einer der Novellen Theodor Storms, der aus Husum stammt.

Quaint old Husum where Theodor Storm was born.

La ville d'Husum où nacquit Theodor Storm.

Fischersiedlung in Schleswig.

Fishing village on the outskirts of Schleswig.

Village de pêcheurs aux alentours de Schleswig.

Schloß Glücksburg in der Landschaft Angeln liegt seit 1920 an der äußersten Nordgrenze Deutschlands.

Glücksburg castle lies in a region called Anglia at the northernmost border of Germany.

Le château de Glücksburg est situé à l'extrémité nord de l'Allemagne d'aujourd'hui.

Das wiedererstandene Kiel, Landeshauptstadt von Schleswig-Holstein. Blick vom Rathausturm über den Kleinen Kiel zur Föhrde.

Kiel, capital of Schleswig-Holstein — a city being reconstructed. View from townhall tower.

Le centre de Kiel, la capitale de Schleswig-Holstein, en cours de réconstruction. Vue de la tour de l'hôtel de ville.

onin

Kripgans

Das Holstentor in Lübeck (1477) ist das Wahrzeichen dieser alten Hansestadt, die einst „Königin der Ostsee" genannt wurde.

The Holstentor in Lübeck (1477), a landmark of this old Hanse town, once called "Queen of the Baltic".

La Holstentor à Lübeck (1477), symbole de cette vieille ville hanséatique, autrefois connue sous le nom de «Reine de la Baltique».

The Bordesholm altar
(1515–21) in Schleswig
cathedral, a masterpiece
of old N. Germany
carving. Detail:
Abraham being
entertained by
Melchisedek.

L'autel de Bordesholm
(1515–21), dans la
cathédrale de Schleswig,
est un chef-d'œuvre
de la sculpture
allemande du nord.
Détail: Abraham
reçoit l'hospitalité
de Melchisédech.

Schirrmann-Hamkens

91   Der Bordesholmer Altar (1515–21), heute im Dom zu Schleswig, ein Meisterwerk der altniederdeutschen Schnitzkunst. Detail: Abraham wird von Melchisedek bewirtet.

„Knicks" überziehen das weite Hügelland in Holstein ebenso wie hier im schleswigschen Angeln.

The rolling hill-country of Holstein is patterned by stone walls overgrown with briar. Angeln, a district of Schleswig.

Le vaste pays accidenté de Holstein ainsi que le pays d'Angeln en Schleswig est traversé par des murs en pierre envahis par le ronce.

Ker

Dodenhoff

Kennzeichen des norddeutschen Küstenlandes zwischen Emden und Flensburg sind noch immer die Windmühlen in weiter Landschaft.

Windmills are typical of the wide, sweeping North German coastal region between Emden and Flensburg.

Les moulins à vent se dressant sur un paysage découvert restent caractéristiques du littoral de l'Allemagne du Nord.

Im Park von Sanssouci bei Potsdam erhebt sich das Sommerschloß Friedrichs des Großen (erbaut 1745–1747).

In the park at Sanssouci: Frederick the Great's summer palace near Potsdam (1745–1747).

Près de Potsdam, le château de Sanssouci (1745–1747), entouré du parc du même nom, était la résidence de Frédéric le Grand.

Neuke

Hartz

BERLIN

ist die eigentliche Hauptstadt
von ganz Deutschland, auch
wenn es seit 1945 von der
westlichen Hälfte des gemein-
samen Vaterlandes getrennt
ist. – Im Jahre 1936 wurde
von der Siegessäule aus dieses Bild der Stadtmitte auf-
genommen. Es wirkt heute
wie eine Fata Morgana, die
eine ferne Welt spiegelt ...

still is the capital of the
whole of Germany – even
though it has been cut off
from the western half of the
country since 1945. In 1936
the picture above of the
center of the city was taken
from "Siegessäule" with a
tele camera. Looking at this
panorama is like seeing a
mirage of a far-away world ...

c'est encore la vraie capitale
de toute l'Allemagne même
que la ville soit séparée de la
partie occidentale de la patrie
commune depuis 1945. – La
photographie ci-dessus fut
prise en 1936 du haut de la
«Siegessäule». Regardant ce
panorame aujourd'hui on se
sent confronté à un mirage,
reflet d'un monde lointain ...

Das Bild des „Schlüterportals" (1716) sei Erinnerung an das Schloß von Berlin, das heute nicht mehr steht.

The Berlin palace of the Hohenzollern kings and emperors with its "Schlüterportal" (1716) is no more.

L'ancien palais impérial de Berlin n'existe plus. Sur la photo: le „Schlüterportal" (1716).

Berlin. Der Französische Dom am Gendarmenmarkt, auch er heute eine Ruine, sei abgebildet als Beispiel für den Preußischen Barock, der dem alten Berlin seinen unverwechselbaren Stempel aufdrückte.

Berlin. The ''French Cathedral'', characteristic example of ''Prussian Baroque'' on Gendarmenmarkt is in ruins today.

Berlin. La «Cathédrale Française», exemple typique du style dit «Baroque Prussien», est en ruines aujourd'hui.

197

Diederle

Das flutende Leben, das Berlin einst auszeichnete, ist heute wenigstens in Westberlin am Kurfürstendamm im Schatten der zerstörten Gedächtniskirche wiederzufinden.

The cosmopolitan life, once characteristic of Berlin, can today be found on Kurfürstendamm in West Berlin. Background: ruins of Kaiser-Wilhelm-Gedächtniskirche.

Berlin. La vie cosmopolite, jadis pulsant dans toute la ville, aujourd'hui a pour centre le Kurfürstendamm, dominé par la Kaiser-Wilhelm-Gedächtniskirche.

Gnilka

Symbol für den Lebenswillen Berlins sind die großen Messen und Ausstellungen, die regelmäßig wieder in den Messehallen veranstaltet werden.

The vitality of present-day Berlin shows itself best in the big fairs and exhibitions regularly taking place in ''Messehallen''.

La vitalité de Berlin d'aujourd'hui se manifeste le mieux dans les foires et expositions qui ont lieu dans les «Messehallen».

Sanssouci (1747), das Schloß Friedrichs des Großen bei Potsdam.

Sanssouci (1747), Frederick the Great's palace near Potsdam.

Sanssouci (1747), le château de Frédéric le Grand, situé près de Potsdam.

Eschen

Potsdam. Die Nikolaikirche, der „Dom" (1849), und davor die Kolonnade des Stadtschlosses (1751).

Potsdam. The Nikolaikirche, called the "cathedral" (1849), and, in the foreground, the colonnade of the town-castle (1751).

Potsdam. La Nikolaikirche, dite la «cathédrale» (1849), et, au premier plan, la colonnade du château de Potsdam (1751).

Rupp

Breite Flußläufe, Seen und Kiefernwälder: Märkisches Land. Blaue Havel im Grunewald.

Wide rivers, lakes, and pine-forests characterise the Mark Brandenburg. The R. Havel in Grunewald.

Cours d'eau, lacs, bois de pin — tout ça caractérise la Marche de Brandebourg. La rivière Havel.

Im Spreewald ersetzen vielfach Wasserläufe die Straßen.

Water-courses replace roads in many parts of the Spreewald.

Des cours d'eau remplacent souvent des routes dans la Spreewald.

Chorin in der Mark. Die Klosterkirche (1334) ist ein bedeutendes Werk der norddeutschen Backsteingotik.

Chorin in the March of Brandenburg. The monastic church (1334) is characteristic of N. German brick Gothic architecture.

Chorin dans la Marche de Brandebourg. L'église (1334) fait honneur à l'architecture gothique en brique du nord de l'Allemagne.

Das Neustädter Tor in Tangermünde a. d. Elbe.

The Neustadt Gate in Tangermünde on the Elbe.

La Porte de Neustadt à Tangermünde s/Elbe

Magdeburg. Der Chor des gotischen Domes. Hier ruhen die Gebeine Ottos des Großen.

Magdeburg. The choir of the Gothic cathedral, containing the remains of Otto the Great.

Magdebourg. Le chœur de la cathédrale gothique où est enterré Otton le Grand.

Strache

Brandenburg, die Keimzelle der Mark, Preußens und des zweiten deutschen Reiches. Das spätgotische Kurfürstenhaus.

Brandenburg, the core of the March, of Prussia, and the Second German Empire. The late Gothic residence of the electors.

Brandebourg, cœur de la Marche, de la Prusse, et du Second Empire Allemand. La résidence gothique des électeurs.

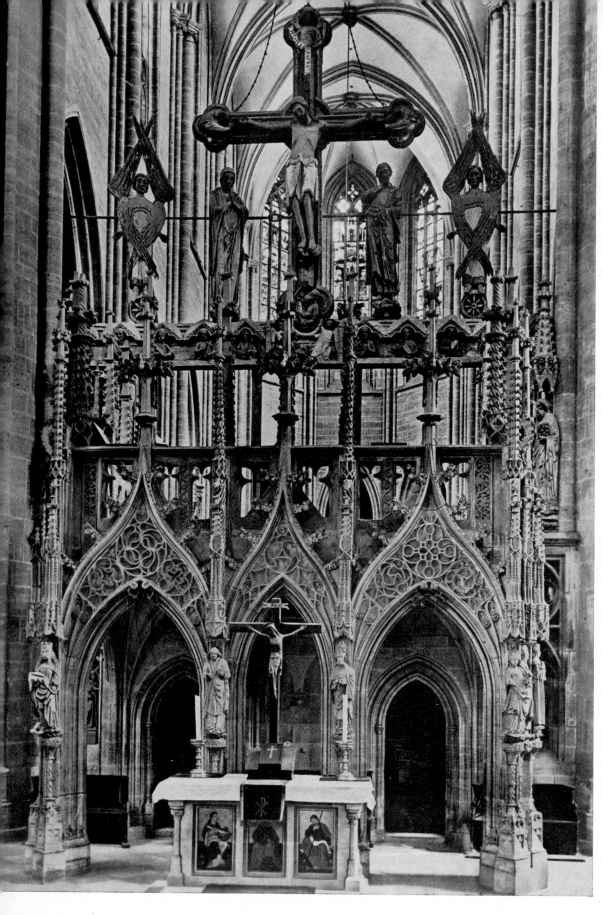

Halberstadt. Der reichgeformte Lettner (1505) des Stephansdomes, darüber das ältere Triumphkreuz (Anfang 13. Jahrh.).

Halberstadt. The choir-screen (1505) of St. Stephen's cathedral with the triumphal cross (early 13th century).

Halberstadt. Le jubé (1505) de la Stephansdom. Au-dessus: la croix triomphale (début du 13e. siècle).

Eisleben, die alte Bergmannstadt südlich des Harzes, Geburts- und Sterbestadt des Reformators Martin Luther (1483–1546).

Eisleben, an old mining town south of the Harz, where Martin Luther was born and died (1483–1546).

Eisleben, vieille ville minière au sud du Harz, lieu de naissance de Martin Luther. Le grand réformateur y mourut en 1546.

„Über allen Gipfeln ist Ruh'..." Im Thüringer Wald entstand dieses Gedicht Goethes.

The wooded hills of Thuringia gave rise to a famous poem by Goethe.

Les collines boisées de la Thuringe ont inspiré un poème célèbre de Goethe.

Nowak

210

Der Name der Wartburg bei Eisenach ist mit denen der hl. Elisabeth und Martin Luthers für ewig verknüpft.

The Wartburg near Eisenach is for ever linked with the names of St. Elizabeth and Martin Luther.

Près d'Eisenach se trouve la célèbre Wartburg dont le nom est inséparable de ceux de Sainte Elisabeth et de Martin Luther.

Das Rathaus am Ring zu Breslau, ein besonders schöner Bürgerbau der späten deutschen Gotik.

Breslau townhall, a specially beautiful civic building, dating from the Late Gothic period.

L'Hôtel de Ville sur la Place du Marché de Breslau, très bel édifice datant de la fin du gothique allemand.

Aufsberg

Mitteldeutsches Land: Blick von der Leuchtenburg ins Saaletal.

Central German landscape: view of the Saale valley taken from Leuchtenburg castle.

Paysage typique de l'Allemagne centrale: la vallée de la Saale vue du château de Leuchtenburg.

Hallensleben

Hoch über Eisenach blickt die Wartburg, ein Symbol für alle Deutschen, weit ins Thüringer Land. Der äußere der beiden Burghöfe.

The Wartburg, lying high above Eisenach, commands a good view of Thuringia. The outer courtyard of the castle with its memories of Luther.

Le château de Wartburg où se réfugia Luther, domine la ville d'Eisenach et tout le pays aux alentours. La cour extérieure du château.

O'Swald-Ruperti

Wie die Wartburg durch Luther, ist Weimar durch Goethe zu einem Symbol für ganz Deutschland geworden. Goethes Gartenhaus.

Through Goethe, Weimar has become a symbol of the true spirit of Germany. Goethe's summer-house.

Grâce à Goethe, la ville de Weimar est devenue symbole de l'esprit allemand. Le pavillon de Goethe.

Erfurt. Dom und Severi-Kirche über den Dächern der einstigen Universitäts- und heutigen Blumenstadt.

The former university town of Erfurt. The cathedral and Severi-Kirche towering over the roofs of the "city of flowers".

Erfurt, ancienne ville universitaire. La cathédrale et la Severi-Kirche qui dominent cette ville de fleurs.

Hege

Naumburg genießt Ruhm durch seinen romanischen Dom mit den herrlichen Plastiken. Die berühmten Stifter Eckehard und Uta (um 1250).

Naumburg is still famous for its Romanesque cathedral. Detail from the choir-screen: the cathedral-founders Eckehard and Uta (ca. 1250).

Naumburg est célèbre par sa cathédrale romane. Détail du jubé: Eckehard et Uta, fondateurs de la cathédrale (c. 1250).

217

R. Müller

Halle an der Saale. Die Marktkirche (1554) der alten Salz- und Universitätsstadt
und das Denkmal des aus Halle stammenden Komponisten Georg Friedrich Händel (1685–1759).

The university town of Halle on the Saale. The Marktkirche (1554) of this old salt-mining town,
and, in front, the monument to George Frederick Händel, a native of Halle.

La ville universitaire de Halle s/Saale. Devant la Marktkirche (1554) de cette vieille ville de salines
se dresse le monument de Georges Frédéric Händel, né à Halle en 1685.

Andres

Leipzig. Das Alte Rathaus der großen mitteldeutschen Buch- und Messestadt.
The old townhall of Leipzig, once centre of the German book trade, and famous for its fairs.
Le vieil hôtel de ville de Leipzig, ville des livres et des foires.

Freiberg im Erzgebirge. Die berühmte Goldene Pforte (um 1240)
am Dom der alten Bergmannstadt.

Freiberg in the Erzgebirge. The famous Golden Portal (ca. 1240)
of the cathedral.

La vieille ville minière de Freiberg dans l'Erzgebirge.
Le célèbre Portal Doré (c. 1240) de la cathédrale.

Annaberg, Stadt des Silberbergbaus. Die spätgotische Hallenkirche St. Anna.

Annaberg. The Late Gothic church of St. Anne in this silver-mining town.

Annaberg. L'église gothique Ste Anne dans cette vieille ville minière.

Gewande

←

Meißen mit Albrechtsburg und Dom über der Elbe.

Meissen. Albrechtsburg and cathedral across the Elbe.

Meissen. Le château d'Albrechtsburg et la cathédrale.

In der Sächsischen Schweiz, dem romantischen Durchbruch der Elbe durch das Elbsandsteingebirge.

In "Saxon Switzerland" — the romantic gorge cut by the Elbe through the mountains.

En «Suisse de Saxe», pays pittoresque où l'Elbe se fraye un chemin à travers les montagnes.

Hallensleben

Der Zwinger in Dresden, 1709–32 für höfische Festaufführungen erbaut (1945 zerstört, seit Jahren im Neuaufbau begriffen),
ist eine der berühmtesten Architekturanlagen der Barockzeit.

The Zwinger in Dresden (1709–32) built for court festivities, was destroyed in 1945. Reconstruction of this most famous Baroque palace is in progress.

Le Zwinger à Dresde (1709–32) destiné aux festins de la cour, fut détruit en 1945.
Depuis des années, on est en train de reconstruire un des palais baroques les plus célèbres.

Dresden, die „Goldene Stadt des Barocks", wie es vor der Zerstörung aussah.

Dresden, the ''Golden Town of Baroque'', before the bombing.

La «ville dorée» de Dresde, riche en trésors baroques. (Vue d'avant-guerre.)

trähle

Schröder

Görlitz an der Neiße wird am schönsten durch die Justitia an seiner alten Rathaustreppe (1537) dokumentiert.

Görlitz on the Neisse. An especially beautiful feature is the figure of Justice on the old staircase of the townhall (1537).

Görlitz sur la Neisse: ce qu'il y a de plus beau, c'est la statue de la Justice qui veille sur le vieil escalier de l'hôtel de ville (1537).

Windstoßer

Die Marienkirche auf der Sandinsel zu Breslau mit reichem Barockschmuck zu spätgotischer Architektur.
A wealth of Baroque ornament over Late Gothic architecture in the Marienkirche on the Sandinsel at Breslau.
Breslau. Les formes pleines de l'art baroque ont laissé des traces sur l'architecture gothique de la Marienkirche.

227

Saebens

R. Müller

Pragher

Das Riesengebirge mit der Schneegrubenbaude bei Oberschreiberhau.

The "Giant Mountains". — The hostel of "Schneegrubenbaude" near Oberschreiberhau.

Les «Monts des Géants». Auberge «Schneegrubenbaude» près d'Oberschreiberhau.

Kloster Leubus an der Oder in Niederschlesien.

Leubus monastery on the Oder in Lower Silesia.

Le monastère de Leubus qui domine l'Oder en Basse-Silésie.

Blick auf den Marktplatz von Frankfurt an der Oder.
View of the market place in Frankfurt on the Oder.
La place du marché de Francfort s/Oder.

Stettin an der Oder, wichtigster Hafen und einst die Hauptstadt Pommerns.

Stettin on the Oder, the most important port and former capital of Pomerania.

Stettin s/Oder, port principal et ancienne capitale de la Poméranie.

Plan und Karte

Der Markt der alten Universitätsstadt Rostock mit St. Marien.

Market place and St. Mary's church in the old university town of Rostock.

La place du marché et l'église Ste Marie de la vieille ville universitaire de Rostock.

Hartz

Greifswald, gleichfalls Universitätsstadt: Rathaus und St. Nikolai.

Greifswald, also a university town: townhall and St. Nikolai.

Greifswald, également ville universitaire: l'hôtel de ville et la Nikolaikirche.

Schwerin. Das neugotische Schloß der Großherzöge von Mecklenburg.

Schwerin. The imitation Gothic castle of the grand dukes of Mecklenburg.

Schwerin. Le château faux gothique des grands ducs de Mecklembourg.

Strähle

Strähle

Stralsund liegt auf einer Insel im Strelasund. Vorn St. Marien, rechts St. Jakobi, oben die Nikolaikirche.

Stralsund is situated on an island in the Strelasund. In the foreground: St. Marien, right: St. Jakobi, above: the Nikolaikirche.

Stralsund est situé sur une île du Strelasund. Au premier plan: Ste Marie, à droite: St Jakobi, aus-dessus: la Nikolaikirche.

Ostsee-Steilküste
beim Wissower Klinken
auf der Insel Rügen.

The rocky
Baltic coastline
on the island of Rügen

Le littoral rocailleux
de la Baltique à Rügen.

Ostpreußen. Der Wachbudenberg an der Samlandküste bei Klein-Kuhren.

The Wachbudenberg in East Prussia near Klein-Kuhren at the Samland coast.

Le Wachbudenberg en Prusse-Orientale près de Klein-Kuhren à la côte de Samland.

Hallensleben

Haustein →

Königsberg. Alte Fachwerkspeicher am Pregelhafen.

Königsberg. Old half-timbered grain-warehouses along the Pregelhafen.

Königsberg. De vieux greniers en cloisonnage le long du Pregelhafen.

Danzig. Die Jopengasse und der Turm der Marienkirche der alten deutschen Hansestadt.

Danzig. Jopengasse and the spire of the Marienkirche.

Danzig, ville vieille hanséatique.

La Jopengasse et la flèche de la Marienkirche (l'église Ste Marie).

240

Maehler

Deutscher Kunstverlag (Grimm) ⟶

Ostpreußische Landschaft.
Blick über die Rominter Heide vom Goldaper Berg aus.

East Prussian landscape. View of the Rominten Heath
from the Goldaper Berg.

Paysage typique de la Prusse-Orientale.
Les landes de Rominten vues de la Goldaper Berg.

Die Marienburg an der Nogat bei Danzig (1274–1448),
von 1309–1427 Sitz der Hochmeister des Deutschen Ritterordens.

The fortress of Marienburg on the R. Nogat near Danzig (1274–1448),
from 1309–1427 the seat of the Grand Master of the Teutonic Order.

La forteresse de Marienburg sur la Nogat près de Danzig (1274–1448)
fut entre 1309 et 1427 siège du Grand-Maître de l'Ordre Teutonique.

Kenner

Die charakteristischen Keitelkähne des Kurischen Haffs.

Barges characteristic of the Kurisches Haff.

Chalands typiques de la Kurisches Haff (région d'étangs).

244